The Country Kitchen
PICNICS
Jean Hatfield

The Country Kitchen

PICNICS

Jean Hatfield

WELDON
PUBLISHING

Front and back of jacket: A perfect picnic spread on an old lace cloth. Left to right: Chinese tea eggs (p. 10), camp pie in the billy (p. 26), soda bread with herbs (p. 39), pickled onions (p. 12), fresh fruit, waldorf coleslaw (p. 34), stuffed roast beef (p. 16), meat juices to accompany the beef, and German potato salad (p. 32).

Page 2: Fruits of summer—plums, cherries and wonderfully fresh lychees. Perfect for the picnic table.

COOK'S NOTES: *Standard spoon and cup measurements are used in all recipes. All spoon and cup measurements are level.*

1 tablespoon = 20 ml spoon
1 teaspoon = 5 ml spoon
1 cup = 250 ml

As the imperial and metric equivalents are not exact, follow either one or the other system of measurement.

All ovens should be preheated to the specified temperature.

Fresh herbs are used unless otherwise stated. If they are unavailable, use half the quantity of dried herbs. Use freshly ground black pepper whenever pepper is used; salt and pepper to taste. Use plain flour unless otherwise stated.

A Kevin Weldon Production
Published by Weldon Publishing,
a division of Kevin Weldon & Associates Pty Ltd
372 Eastern Valley Way, Willoughby, NSW 2068 Australia

First Published 1992

© Copyright Kevin Weldon & Associates Pty Ltd
© Copyright design: Kevin Weldon & Associates Pty Ltd

Publishing Manager: Robin Burgess
Project Coordinator: Barbara Beckett
Designer and illustrator: Barbara Beckett
Photographer: Ray Jarratt
Typeset in Hong Kong by Graphicraft Typesetters Ltd
Produced in Hong Kong by Mandarin Offset

National Library of Australia Cataloguing-in-Publication
Data:
Hatfield, Jean.
  Picnics
ISBN 1 875410 62 7
1. Outdoor cookery.   2. Picnicking.   I. Title. (Series: Country Kitchen).
641.578

CONTENTS

PICNICS FOR PLEASURE

OF ALL the occasions in which eating counts for something, a picnic must be the most enjoyable. After deciding on a shady spot, surrounded by soft grass and preferably near a running stream or seashore, it is now up to the host to decide on the menu and whether the guests will be asked to assist with the provisions. This is often advisable, as fresh air sharpens the appetite and makes everything taste especially good. So do allow for this.

Before we start preparing the food for a picnic, we have to think how we are going to transport it. Here are a number of aids to a successful picnic:

Ice packs are available in two sizes and if frozen completely will stay cold for about four hours. To freeze, place in the freezer compartment of the refrigerator for eight to ten hours. They should be placed in plastic bags before putting them into the picnic basket or box so that condensation doesn't come in contact with the food. Ice packs are excellent for using in insulated bags in which you carry bottles of drink. They will not rust and can be reused over and over again.

Vacuum flasks. Most department stores carry a range of vacuum flasks in different sizes. The tall, thin one is still the most popular one for carrying drinks and soup, and the wide-necked style is good for carrying ice or hot dishes. When using a flask for hot liquids, fill it first with hot (but not boiling) water, put the top on, and leave it for fifteen minutes. Empty the water out, then pour in the piping hot liquid. If the flask is to be used to carry cold drinks or ice, fill it first with ice-cold water.

Insulated bags and boxes are marvellous for transporting hot or cold food and keeping it at the right temperature.

Paper plates and cups are a godsend if you have children. But remember they are never as strong as plastic or china.

Polythene bags come in every size and shape and are useful for wrapping cutlery and ice packs and, most of all, for carrying home your rubbish.

Bubble wrap. Polythene bubble wrap is usually found wrapped round such diverse things as electric appliances or in chocolate boxes or protecting fine china. Don't throw it away, as it is good for insulating food, either hot or cold.

Picnic baskets. A wicker picnic hamper certainly adds a note of grandeur to the occasion. However, it can be very heavy when packed. In any case, few households own one. An excellent substitute is a small plastic clothes basket, preferably one with handles. If a shopping basket is used, check that it has a flat bottom and a sturdy handle.

When packing the picnic basket, start with the cold food at the bottom and, if necessary, have the basket lined with a towel; then put in the cold packs.

Make a list of dishes, plates, cutlery, etc., and as each goes in the basket cross it off.

Pack the plates vertically down the sides of the basket with paper napkins between them.

FISH AND STARTERS

Potted Prawns

Potted prawns are simple to prepare and are easily carried in recycled yoghurt or cream cheese containers. I often use royal reds for this dish, as they are usually cheaper than other prawns.

500 g (1 lb) prawns (peeled weight) or 1 kg
(2 lb) whole prawns
185 g (6 oz) butter
¼ teaspoon ground mace
¼ teaspoon nutmeg
A pinch of cayenne
1 teaspoon ground mixed spice
Pepper

Cut the prawns into 2 or 3 pieces. Melt the butter in a large frying pan and when the foam subsides add the prawns and the mace, nutmeg, cayenne, mixed spice and pepper. Toss in the butter for a few minutes.

Spoon or pour into 4 small containers or 1 large tub. Press lightly, then cover with a round piece of aluminium foil and chill in the refrigerator. Serve with Melba toast or crackers.

Camp-Fire Fishcakes

I always have a packet of instant mashed potato and a can of tuna in my cupboard, for these fishcakes are a great favourite when picnicking or sailing because of the ease in preparation.

A 4-serving packet of instant mashed potato
60 g (2 oz) butter or margarine
4 teaspoons finely chopped chives
200 g (6 oz) can tuna or salmon
A squeeze of lemon juice
Salt and pepper
1 egg, beaten
1 cup dry breadcrumbs
Oil or butter for frying

Prepare the potatoes according to the package directions, and beat in the butter and chives.

Remove any bones and skin from the tinned fish, then flake. Combine with the potatoes, and season to taste with lemon juice, salt and pepper. Form the mixture into cakes, dip them in beaten egg and then in breadcrumbs. Fry in a little oil or butter until nicely browned.

Serve with mayonnaise or lemon wedges. Serves 4.

Smoked Trout with Horseradish Cream

Smoked trout, which is available at most good food stores and fish markets, makes the most delicious and beautiful salad. When taking it on a picnic, carry the vegetables in a plastic bag, the fillets of trout on a plate and the dressing in a screw-top jar.

3 smoked trout or 1 larger smoked sea trout
6 tablespoons sour cream
2 tablespoons bottled horseradish
Salad greens, including several lettuces,
watercress, and, if liked, steamed
asparagus or snow peas

Camp-fire fishcakes are easy to make and tempting to eat. They are being prepared here from a tin of pink salmon.

DRESSING

1 tablespoon olive oil
1 tablespoon walnut oil
2 teaspoons balsamic or wine vinegar
A few twists of the pepper mill

Skin the trout and fillet them by running a knife down the centre of each and lifting strips off carefully. Place the fillets on a plate, cover with plastic film, and refrigerate until required.

Lightly mix the sour cream and horseradish. Place in a jar.

Pick over the salad greens, reserving the tender, young and perfect leaves, wash, spin dry and store in a plastic bag in the refrigerator. Steam or blanch in boiling salted water the green asparagus or snow peas; drain and keep aside.

Combine the dressing ingredients in a small screw-top jar.

When ready to serve, place the salad vegetables in a bowl, shake the dressing, pour it over, and toss. Pass round the trout fillets with the horseradish cream. Serves 6 to 8.

*Leave the shells on the Chinese tea eggs until you
reach your picnic spot. Children enjoy helping to
break the shells.*

Chinese Tea Eggs

These spiced eggs with their beautiful
marbled appearance resembling antique
porcelain are ideal for handing round in
their shells while you are preparing the
picnic.

12 eggs
3 tablespoons black tea
1 tablespoon salt
A strip of mandarin peel
6 cloves star anise
½ cup soy sauce

Place the eggs in a saucepan and cover
with cold water. Bring to the boil and
allow to cook gently for 10 minutes.
Remove the eggs and reserve the

10

cooking water. Cool the eggs thoroughly under cold running water. Tap each cooled egg lightly all over with a spoon, cracking the shell but leaving it entire. Add the tea, salt, mandarin peel, anise and soy sauce to the reserved water and bring it to the boil. Gently lower the cracked eggs into the spiced water, cover and simmer gently until the eggs turn brown—about 40 minutes. Remove from heat and allow to stand covered until cold. Refrigerate until ready to serve. Remove shells and cut into quarters if preferred.

Escabeche

This is an excellent dish if the fishermen in your family have had a good catch and you have no room in the freezer. I often make it for Sunday lunch in the park, as it benefits from being made in advance. Use any kind of white fish fillets, such as bream, mirror dory, flathead or whiting.

1 kg (2 lb) fish fillets

BATTER
1 cup flour
A pinch of salt
1 tablespoon oil
1 cup water
1 teaspoon vinegar

SAUCE
1 cup dry white wine
¾ cup olive oil
¾ cup white wine vinegar
1 teaspoon mustard
Pepper and salt to taste
1 red onion, sliced thinly
4 gherkins, sliced thinly
8 green olives

8 black olives
1 tablespoon capers
1 lemon, thinly sliced

Trim the fillets and cut into small serving pieces. Dust with flour, salt and pepper.

Sift the flour and salt into a basin, make a well in centre of the flour and beat in the oil, water and vinegar to make a fairly thin batter. Dip the floured fillets in the batter and deep fry in oil until golden brown. Drain fillets on crumpled paper and allow to cool.

Make a sauce by combining the wine, oil and vinegar seasoned with the mustard and pepper and salt. Beat until combined, then fold in the onion and gherkins. Place the cooled fish in a serving bowl and spoon over the sauce. Decorate with olives, capers and the thinly sliced lemon. Let it stand for at least 2 hours before serving. It will keep in the refrigerator for several days. Serves 4.

Mushrooms Coriander

The combined flavours of the orange-scented coriander and the bay leaves give a wonderful taste to this dish. It is served cold and can be stored in the refrigerator for a few days.

500 g (1 lb) small white mushrooms
Juice of 1 lemon
2 teaspoons coriander seeds
4 tablespoons olive oil
3 bay leaves
Salt
Pepper

Clean the mushrooms with a cloth dipped in water and lemon juice. Trim the stalks. Slice the mushrooms into quarters and squeeze some lemon juice over them.

Crush the coriander seeds in a mortar or with a rolling pin. Heat the olive oil in a heavy frying pan over a low heat. Add the coriander seeds and allow to heat through. Add the mushrooms and bay leaves. Season with salt and pepper. Cook 1 minute. Cover the pan and allow the mushrooms to cook for a further 5 minutes over a very low heat.

Place the mushrooms in a lidded bowl and cool. Serve with crusty French bread to mop up the juices.

Pickled Onions

Whether eaten with cold meat or cheese, there is nothing quite so appetising as a home-made pickled onion.

1.5 kg (3 lb) small white onions
1 cup salt
Water
1½ cups white sugar
12 cloves
2 tablespoons peppercorns
3 cups white vinegar

Cut off the ends of the onions neatly, peel them, and place them in a glass bowl. Dissolve the salt in about 8 cups of water and pour over the onions. Be sure they are completely covered. Place a piece of plastic film on top of the bowl and cover with a small plate or saucer. This will keep the onions submerged. Leave to stand for 18 to 24 hours.

Place the sugar, cloves, peppercorns and vinegar in a stainless steel or enamelled saucepan and bring slowly to the boil. Remove from heat, cover, and let stand for 12 to 18 hours. Drain the onions and rinse well. Pack into jars and cover with strained spiced vinegar. You can leave a few cloves and peppercorns in the vinegar, but too many will produce a very murky appearance. Cover and leave for a month.

Brown pickled onions are made in the same way, but use brown sugar and brown vinegar, and for a pretty effect place a hot chilli in each jar.

Pickled onions are always a popular choice. They are very quick and easy to make.

SAVOURY PASTRY

Cornish Pasties

In Cornwall they say, 'The Devil and all goes into a pasty.' We have used fresh meat, potato and turnip to fill our pasties, and very popular they are on a chilly winter's day. Taken straight from the oven and wrapped in foil, they will stay warm for several hours.

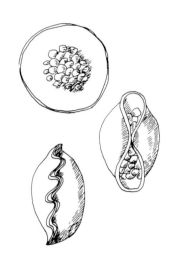

2 cups flour
A pinch of salt
½ teaspoon baking powder
125 g (4 oz) butter or margarine
3 tablespoons cold water
375 kg (12 oz) round or topside steak
2 medium potatoes
1 small turnip
1 onion
Salt and pepper
Stock or water
1 egg, beaten

Sift the flour, salt and baking powder into a bowl. Rub in the butter or margarine and mix with enough water to make a firm dough. Chill for at least 30 minutes before using. Roll out the pastry thinly and cut into rounds, using a 13 cm (5 in.) plate or saucepan lid as a guide. Cut the steak into small strips. Peel and thinly slice the potatoes, turnip and onion.

On one half of the pastry circle place a layer of potato, then turnip, onion and lastly meat, seasoning each layer with salt and pepper. Repeat layers with the onion next to the meat and the potato on the outside, again seasoning each layer. Damp the edges of the circle and fold the uncovered half over the mound of filling, leaving a margin of pastry on the covered half to turn up over the edge of the top half and crimp into a frill from one point of the pasty to the other. This makes a good seal when completed, but it should not be completed until you have raised the open end of the pasty and poured in about 2 tablespoons of stock or water to make the gravy—more if you can, for a goodish bit of gravy in a meat pasty is highly prized. It soaks into the potatoes and spreads the flavours.

Many Cornish women turn the pasty so that its folded and crimped edge runs across the top like a cockscomb. However, flat pasties can be more useful when packing a basket.

Brush with the beaten egg and bake on a tray in a hot oven (220°C; 430°F) for 20 minutes, then lower the heat to moderate (180°C; 360°F) and bake for a further 10 minutes. Makes 6 to 8 pasties.

Hunza Pie

With its moist filling and dry crust, this pie is excellent transportable fare. It is popular with teenagers and vegetarians and can be served warm or cold. I find the best way to carry it is wrapped in a clean tea-towel fastened with sticky tape.

PASTRY
2 cups wholemeal flour
1 teaspoon salt
1 cup wheat germ
180 g (6 oz) butter or margarine
¼ cup water (approx.)

FILLING
1.25 kg (2½ lb) potatoes, peeled
½ bunch spinach
1 tablespoon oil
2 tablespoons yoghurt
Salt

Sift the flour and salt into a bowl; add the husks left in the sifter to the flour. Add the wheat germ and mix lightly. Rub in the butter until the mixture resembles breadcrumbs. Add enough water to mix to a firm dough, then turn out onto a lightly floured surface and knead lightly.

Divide the pastry in halves and roll out one half to line the bottom of a 23 cm (9 in.) pie plate. Store in the refrigerator. Cut the potatoes into quarters and cook in lightly salted

COOK'S NOTES: *Don't forget to take some basic necessities on picnics, such as a groundsheet or rug, insect repellent, blockout cream; corkscrew, tin opener, sharp knives, matches, glasses, plates, cutlery, salt, pepper, sugar and sauces. Clean up the picnic area before you leave, and carry out your rubbish, leaving the area in a pristine state for the next picnicker.*

water for 10 minutes. Drain well and mash lightly. Wash and drain the spinach, and cut into shreds; put into a saucepan with the oil and gently heat through. Combine the potatoes, drained spinach, yoghurt and salt to taste, and mix well. Allow to cool.

Spoon the filling into the pastry case, packing down well. Roll out the remaining pastry to cover the pie dish. Trim and decorate the edges. Brush with water and make a few air vents in the top of pastry. Bake in a hot oven (200°C; 400°F) for 15 minutes or until the pastry is golden brown, then reduce heat to moderate (180°C; 360°F) and cook for a further 15 minutes or until the pastry is nicely brown and crisp. Serves 6 to 8.

COOK'S NOTES: *Fresh air sharpens the appetite, so take more food than you normally eat to satisfy everyone.*

Salmon en Croute

For sheer luxury, this dish reigns supreme. Served with a bowl of rémoulade sauce or home-made mayonnaise, this will be the most remembered picnic dish, worthy of the Opera in the Park or Glyndebourne. Ask your fish shop to skin and fillet a large tail piece of salmon.

1 kg (2 lb) tail piece salmon, skinned and filleted
2 tablespoons fresh chopped chives
A few sprigs of fresh sorrel or parsley or dill, chopped
Juice of 1 small lemon
2 × 375 g (12 oz) packs frozen puff pasty, thawed
2 tablespoons semolina
1 egg, beaten
Salt and ground black pepper

RÉMOULADE SAUCE
2 egg yolks
⅔ cup extra virgin olive oil
⅔ cup sunflower oil
2 tablespoons white wine vinegar
1 teaspoon Dijon mustard
2 tablespoons capers, chopped
1 tablespoon gherkins, chopped
1 tablespoon fresh chopped parsley

Season the salmon fillets and flavour
with the herbs and lemon juice. Lay
them on top of one another.

Roll out one pastry piece to a shape
about 4 cm (1½ in.) larger all round
than the fish. Prick it well and place it
on a baking tray. Bake at 200°C (400°F)
for 15 minutes until golden brown. If it
has risen, then press it down. Sprinkle
over the semolina, and brush the edges
with beaten egg. Lay the fish on top.
Roll out the remaining pastry so that it
is large enough to completely overlap.
Fit over the top and press well to seal.
Trim the edges and crimp.

If you want to decorate the pie,
re-roll any trimmings and cut out long
thin strips. Brush the pie all over with
more egg, then make a lattice pattern
on top with the strips. Return to the
oven and bake for 15 minutes, then
reduce the heat to 180°C (360°F) for a
further 40 minutes, checking to see the
pastry doesn't burn.

Cool, then loosen the base with a
thin palette knife and transfer the pie
onto a thin board.

Make the sauce as you would a
mayonnaise, in a food processor or by
hand, beating the oil gradually into the
egg yolks mixed with some seasoning.
When thick and creamy, add the
remaining ingredients.

Serve the pie in thin slices, and the
sauce separately. Serves 6 to 8.

COLD MEATS

Glazed Pumped Leg of Mutton

If you are fortunate enough in finding
a butcher who still sells mutton or
hogget, do try this delicious recipe. If
mutton is unavailable, get him to pump
a leg of lamb or a piece of veal; it is
easily done in a cryovac pack. This is an
excellent dish for a picnic or outdoor
event.

1 pumped leg of mutton or lamb
½ cup orange juice
¼ cup port wine
1 tablespoon prepared English mustard
¼ cup shredded orange marmalade

Have the shank sawn on the leg so that
it will fit into your boiler. Place in a
large boiler, cover with fresh cold
water, and bring to a simmer. Cover
and simmer gently (do not boil) for 1 to
1¼ hours for lamb, 1¾ to 2 hours for
mutton.

Leave to cool in the liquid, drain and
refrigerate in a sealed container until
required.

Place the meat in a baking dish and
make shallow cuts diagonally across the
joint. Mix the orange juice, port and
mustard and brush over the meat. Bake
in a moderate oven (180°C; 360°F) for
30 minutes, basting frequently with the
glaze. Add a little stock to the baking
dish to prevent scorching. Spread the
meat with marmalade. Cook till the
glaze bubbles and remove from the
oven.

Cool and serve with salads. Serves 6
to 8.

15

Rare Lamb with Hazelnut Dressing

You can either cook the lamb especially for this dish or use the remains of a leg of lamb. This is a particularly good mixture of flavours, but if hazelnut oil is not obtainable, use walnuts and walnut oil.

1 kg (2 lb) lean rolled leg or shoulder of lamb
Salt and ground black pepper
3 tablespoons hazelnut oil
125 g (4 oz) shelled hazelnuts, lightly toasted and chopped
1 medium onion, ideally red, sliced thinly
125 g (4 oz) thin green beans, tailed, halved and lightly cooked

Season the lamb lightly, roast at 190°C (375°F), for about 45 to 50 minutes. Cool, cut into thin slices and then shreds. Mix in a bowl with the oil and nuts, and check the seasoning.

Meanwhile, soak the onion slices in cold water for about 2 hours. Mix with the lamb and nuts and the cooked beans. Cover and chill for a further 2 hours, or overnight, then cover ready for transporting. Serves 6 to 8.

COOK'S NOTES: *Remember, 'One flaming match, no flaming trees.' Before lighting a fire, check that there are no current fire bans. Clean up the picnic site, making sure there are no hot coals left or glass which can concentrate heat and create bushfires.*

Stuffed Roast Beef

This is a favourite dish with Italian families to take on a picnic. It looks very attractive when carved in thin slices and stays moist and succulent.

1 kg (2 lb) flank or skirt steak
1 carrot
1 onion
1 stalk celery
4 chicken livers
2 cups breadcrumbs
½ cup grated parmesan cheese
1 egg
1 teaspoon chopped basil or thyme
Salt and pepper to taste
125 g (4 oz) salami sausage
½ cup chopped parsley
Oil for frying
Stock, water or wine

Flatten out the steak—it will be easier if it has been first plunged into cold water for a minute. Prepare the stuffing by chopping the carrot, onion, celery and livers—this can be done in a blender. Add the breadcrumbs, grated cheese and egg and season to taste with herbs, salt and pepper.

Spread the stuffing on top of the flattened meat. Remove the skin from the salami, cut into thin slices and lay them over the top, roll and sprinkle with parsley. Tie with string. Heat a little oil in a heavy casserole dish or saucepan, and brown the roll gently. Add a little stock, water or wine, cover with greased paper and a lid, and cook very gently for about 2 hours, turning occasionally.

Remove the rolled meat from the pot and strain the gravy into a bowl. Wrap the roll in foil and, when sufficiently cool, store in the refrigerator. For a special occasion, remove the fat from the top of the gravy and slightly melt the jelly remaining in the basin, then brush it over the roll before carving it into thin slices.

Stuffed roast beef is not expensive to make and looks and tastes like a grand dish.

Devilled Cutlets

These delicious cutlets should be grilled just before departure for the picnic and packed in foil containers. They will be still warm on arrival if you don't have to travel too far.

8 lamb cutlets
1 teaspoon each salt, dry mustard, ground
*   ginger, garam masala*
2 teaspoons sugar
2 tablespoons each tomato relish, fruit
*   chutney*
1 tablespoon Worcestershire sauce
30 g (1 oz) butter

Trim the cutlets and rub them well with the dried spices (mixed together) and sugar—you will find the back of a teaspoon does the job. Leave for at least 1 hour, or preferably overnight. Under a preheated grill, cook for 3 minutes on each side. Combine the relish, chutney and sauce and spread over the cutlets; cook a further 2 minutes on each side. Pack for the picnic along with paper napkins to hold the cutlets.

Garam Masala

Although commercially prepared garam masala is available from various food outlets, you can make your own by combining 2 teaspoons of cumin seeds, 1 teaspoon of black peppercorns, $\frac{1}{2}$ teaspoon of whole cloves, a 2–3 cm piece of cinnamon stick and 4 bay leaves in a blender and blend for 1 minute or until the ingredients are reduced to a power. Store in a screw-top jar.

Spiced Beef

Many nationalities class beef as their favourite cold meat; this dish should satisfy these beef fanciers. It can be made a few days ahead and cut either into thin slices if it is to be served at table or in thin strips if it is to be eaten alfresco.

3 kg (6 lb) corner topside, rump or bolar
*   blade*
2 onions, sliced
1 stick celery, chopped
1 bay leaf
1 teaspoon ground cinnamon
1 teaspoon allspice
6 whole cloves
1 teaspoon salt
1 teaspoon crushed peppercorns
1 cup wine vinegar or red wine
2 tablespoons olive oil

Trim any excess fat from the beef, place in a china or plastic bowl and add the sliced onions, chopped celery, bay leaf, cinnamon, allspice, cloves, salt, peppercorns and vinegar or wine. Cover and refrigerate overnight, turning the beef occasionally.

Drain the beef and reserve the marinade. Pat the joint with paper towels. Heat the oil in a roasting pan and brown the meat on all sides. Heat the reserved marinade and pour it over the beef. Cover the roasting pan with foil, tucking the foil round the edge, or, if available, use a lidded casserole. Cook in a slow oven (160°C; 320°F) for about 2 to 2½ hours or until a fine skewer inserted into the thickest part of the meat comes out easily. Don't overcook or it will crumble when carved. Take the joint from the liquid, wrap it in the foil covering, place in a shallow dish, cover with a board and weight it

down—canned fruit tins are good as weights. When cool, store in the refrigerator.

When ready to serve, combine 1 cup of vinaigrette dressing, $\frac{1}{2}$ cup chopped parsley, 1 tablespoon Dijon mustard, $\frac{1}{4}$ cup salted capers and some finely chopped tiny sour gherkins. Slice the beef thinly and arrange slices in an overlapping pattern in shallow platters. Pour the herbed vinaigrette over the sliced beef. The dish is improved if allowed to marinate for an hour or two before serving.

Serves 25 to 30.

Spiced beef makes a special occasion of a picnic lunch or dinner. Serve it with a leafy salad and dill pickles.

Cobb Salad

This salad, made famous at the Brown Derby Restaurant in Hollwood, is a satisfying and tasty one-dish meal, particularly easy to make now that chicken breasts are so available. You can substitute mignonette lettuce if witloof is out of season. Take the dressing to the picnic in a jar and arrange the salad in a large bowl.

Chicken salad is a particularly popular picnic dish. There never seems to be enough of it.

½ head iceberg lettuce, torn into pieces
1 head witloof, leaves separated
1 cup watercress sprigs or arugula
2 tomatoes, finely diced
2 poached chicken breasts, diced
2 hard-boilded eggs, chopped
1 green pepper, diced
2 rashers bacon, crisply cooked and crumbed
1 avocado, finely chopped
6 spring onions, finely chopped
3 tablespoons grated romano or parmesan cheese
Paprika dressing

In a large serving bowl, make a bed of lettuce; arrange the witloof around and then the watercress or arugula. Arrange the remaining ingredients, except for the dressing, in bundles or distinct layers in any order; cover. Chill for 30 minutes or until ready to serve, then toss the salad with the dressing. Serves 6 to 8.

PAPRIKA DRESSING: Put in a lidded jar 1 tablespoon each of honey, water and Dijon mustard, add 2 teaspoons paprika and ½ teaspoon salt and shake well. Add ½ cup pure olive oil and 1 tablespoon vinegar, and shake well just before using.

Chicken Salad

A variation of the traditional party dish and America's favourite salad. Since it is made with mayonnaise, take care to refrigerate it, particularly if made in advance, and don't carry it in the boot of the car if travelling any distance.

8 half breasts of chicken
4 cups chicken stock
2 sticks celery, finely chopped
Salt and freshly ground white pepper
2 tablespoons chopped tarragon or 2
*   teaspoons dried*
½ cup sour cream
½ cup mayonnaise
4 spring onions, finely chopped

Place the chicken breasts in a large frying pan or flameproof dish. Add the chicken stock, celery and salt and pepper to taste. Bring the liquid to a simmer and cook the chicken gently for 10 minutes. Remove from heat and allow the chicken to cool in the liquid for 20 minutes. Place the tarragon in a large bowl, pour ¼ cup of the hot poaching liquid over; leave for 15 minutes; then stir in the sour cream and mayonnaise.

Remove the chicken from the liquid, discard skin and bones and separate the meat into slivers. Fold into the sauce with spring onions, with salt and pepper to taste. Chill. Serve with a tossed salad.

VARIATION: WALDORF CHICKEN SALAD: Add 1 diced apple, ½ cup chopped pecan nuts and an additional ¼ cup mayonnaise.

COOK'S NOTES: *Picnic menus can be highly imaginative, but do remember the dishes should be easy to transport and not too cumbersome.*

Jellied Chicken Loaf

In this recipe the pig's trotter is optional, but it does give extra flavour and helps set the jelly. Decorate the bottom of the mould with chopped parsley.

1.5 kg (3 lb) chicken
1 pig's trotter (optional)
2 tablespoons dry white wine or lemon juice
1 onion, peeled
1 carrot, scraped
1 stalk celery
1 bay leaf
A strip of lemon rind
6 peppercorns
2 teaspoons salt
3 teaspoons gelatine

Place all ingredients except the gelatine in a large saucepan. Cover with water and bring slowly to the boil. Skim, then cover and simmer gently 1 to 1½ hours or until chicken is tender. Remove pan from heat and allow to cool a little. Strain 2½ cups of liquid from the saucepan and season to taste. Sprinkle gelatine on top, stir briskly and set aside.

Carefully remove the chicken flesh from the carcass and put the bones aside with the skin. Cut the flesh into thin strips. It is important that the chicken is tender.

Decorate the bottom of a terrine mould by pouring a little of the jellied stock into the base and allowing it almost to set, then place gherkins, cut like a fan, and sliced stuffed olives on top. Cover with a little more jellied stock and allow it to set before arranging the strips of chicken on top of that. Fill up the mould with the remaining chicken and the chopped flesh of the pig's trotter if used. Pour the remaining jellied stock over the meat and refrigerate. Serves 6 to 8.

Herbed Meat Loaf

Skim milk powder and wheat germ add extra nourishment to this herb-flavoured, high-protein loaf.

2 tablespoons olive oil
1 clove garlic, crushed
1 small red or green capsicum (pepper), finely chopped
500 g (1 lb) lean minced beef, lamb or veal
2 eggs, beaten
⅓ cup powdered skim milk
⅓ cup wheat germ
3 tablespoons chopped fresh herbs (parsley, thyme, marjoram, etc.) or ½ teaspoon dried herbs chopped into 2 tablespoons of parsley
Salt and pepper to taste
Paprika

Heat the oil in a frying pan, and gently fry the garlic, capsicum and onion until soft. Combine with the remaining ingredients, except paprika, in a bowl, then pack into a greased loaf tin and sprinkle the top with paprika. Bake in a preheated moderate oven (180°C; 360°F) for 1 hour. Remove from the oven and allow to cool. Refrigerate until ready to use.

COOK'S NOTES: *Children like individual lunch boxes, so put in a few surprises and enjoy a hassle-free picnic.*

Luncheon Sausage

A moist, tasty meat-and-vegetable loaf, very transportable. Serve with carrot and pecan salad (page 37) and German potato salad (page 32).

⅓ cup chopped onion
2 tablespoons chopped capsicum (green pepper)
2 tablespoons butter or margarine
2 eggs, beaten
⅓ cup tomato juice
½ cup rolled oats
1 teaspoon salt
¼ teaspoon dry mustard
750 g (1½ lb) minced beef steak
250 g (8 oz) pork mince

Set the oven at 180°C (360°F).

Cook the onion and capsicum in butter or margarine until soft but not brown. Combine the eggs with the tomato juice, rolled oats, salt and mustard.

Add the egg mixture to the cooked vegetables. Add the meat and mix well. Pat the mixture into a loaf tin.

Bake for 1½ hours. Remove from the oven and place a board and weight on top. A can of fruit makes a good weight. When cool, store in the refrigerator and take to the picnic in the loaf tin. Serves 8.

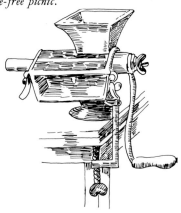

Orange Meat Loaf

An easy dish to handle at a picnic.
Serve with potato salad (page 32).

750 g (1½ lb) minced steak
¼ cup orange juice
1 egg
1½ cups fresh white breadcrumbs
1 onion, finely chopped
1 teaspoon salt
¼ teaspoon nutmeg
¼ teaspoon pepper
2 teaspoons chopped parsley
1 teaspoon dried thyme

TOPPING
¼ cup tomato paste
⅓ cup firmly packed brown sugar
¼ teaspoon dry mustard
¼ teaspoon cinnamon
¼ teaspoon ground cardamom or cloves
3 slices orange, halved

Combine all the meat loaf ingredients
and mix well. Lightly pack into a
greased loaf tin. Bake in a preheated
moderate oven (180°C; 360°F), on the
lower shelf for 30 minutes.

TOPPING
Combine the tomato paste, sugar,
mustard and spices and mix well. Place
the orange slices on top of the meat
loaf, spoon the spice mixture over, and
bake for a further 30 minutes or until
cooked and the top nicely glazed. When
cool, store in refrigerator.

*Overleaf: A picnic lunch for four. Left to right:
barley lemonade (p. 47), carrot cookies (p. 42),
citrus tea bread (p. 41), lamb kebabs (p. 31),
orange meat loaf (p. 23), chicken salad (p. 21),
and carrot salad (p. 37).*

*Orange meat loaf looks spectacular with its
tomato glaze brushed over the orange slices.*

Camp pie always inspires cries of admiration at a picnic. It is very practical and easy to make.

Camp Pie

When my family came to Australia from Scotland we very quickly became Australians and took to having picnics in the bush, but my mother had difficulty coming to grips with the 'billy'. Although the *Macquarie Dictionary* defines a billy as a cylindrical container for liquids having a close-fitting lid, the word probably coming from the Scots *bally* (a milk pail), it was certainly not used in Scotland. However, it was not very long before Mother was cooking Aberdeen sausage in a billy, and to this day I find it is the best way of cooking and transporting this favourite picnic dish. My friends have renamed it camp pie, though it is a vast improvement on the canned food of that name.

250 g (8 oz) bacon, rind removed
750 g (1½ lb) topside steak, minced
1 cup soft, white breadcrumbs
3 teaspoons Worcestershire sauce
1 tablespoon chopped parsley
Grated rind of ½ lemon
Salt and pepper to taste
1 egg, beaten

Chop the bacon finely and combine

26

with the minced steak, breadcrumbs and seasonings. Add the beaten egg, mix well and pack the mixture into a well-greased billycan. Cover with buttered paper, press down into the can, and cover with a well-fitting lid. Gently steam for 2 hours. When cooked, remove the lid and place a weight on top of the meat—a large can of fruit just fits—and leave until cool. Then refrigerate overnight or until well chilled. You can either remove the sausage from the can, slice it with a sharp knife and return it to the can or slice it at the picnic. Don't forget the lid. Serves 6 to 8.

out, remove the remaining bones, and trim off the root. Slit the underside of the skin and remove it. The skin should come off easily if you push your thumbs underneath it to ease the edges, then peel it off.

To press an oxtongue, curve the tongue into a deep cake tin or soufflé dish which seems almost too small for it. Put a small plate on top of the tongue and weight it down with a heavy object such as a large can of fruit. Leave it in a cool place overnight. When the tongue is turned out, it will be tightly compacted and easy to carve in thin slices.

Tongue

Cold tongue is a lovely picnic dish. If pickled or smoked tongue has been heavily salted (ask the butcher), it must be blanched before cooking. To do this, cover the tongue with cold water, bring very slowly to the boil and then drain.

TO COOK: Place the tongue (fresh, salted or smoked) in a saucepan and cover it with cold water. For 1 oxtongue or 6 to 8 lambs' tongues, add 6 whole allspice, 6 whole cloves, 6 black peppercorns, a bouquet garni, 1 sliced onion, 1 sliced carrot and 1 sliced stalk of celery. Add 1½ teaspoons of salt if cooking fresh tongue. Bring slowly to the boil, skim the surface and simmer, covered, for about 3 hours for oxtongue and 1 to 1½ hours for lamb's tongues.

The boiled tongue is cooked when one of the small bones near the root end can be easily pulled out. Let it stand in the liquid until it is cool enough to handle, then take the tongue

Potted Tongue

I love this picnic dish and usually cook two tongues at a time, curling one into a dish and pressing to enjoy sliced, and treating the other this way.

250 g (8 oz) cooked salted oxtongue
90 g (3 oz) ghee or butter
¼ teaspoon ground nutmeg
Freshly ground black or white pepper
Extra ghee for sealing

Remove any fat, gristle or skin from the tongue and cut the meat into pieces. Place in a food processor fitted with the steel blade, add the 90 g of ghee and process until smooth. Beat in the nutmeg and a little pepper, then pack into a pot or pots, smoothing the top. Chill until firm. Melt the extra ghee and pour over the surface to cover and seal. Cover pots with foil and store in the refrigerator.

Serve chilled with Melba toast or with crusty bread and crisp raw vegetables for a great picnic dish. Makes about 2 cups.

Danish Liver Pâté

Liver pâté, home-made or bought, is excellent used for Danish open sandwiches made at the picnic. You can use lamb, chicken, pork or duck liver; I prefer duck.

375 g (12 oz) liver
125 g (4 oz) streaky bacon rashers
5 anchovy fillets
1¼ cup milk
1 bay leaf
1 onion, sliced
A few peppercorns
30 g (1 oz) butter or margarine
2 tablespoons flour
Salt and pepper
1 egg, beaten
60 g (2 oz) melted butter or ghee for the
*   top of pâté*

Slice the livers and snip away any cores. Trim and chop the bacon rashers. Mince these and the anchovy fillets, using a coarse blade, or blend in a food processor. Meanwhile, put the milk, bay leaf, onion and peppercorns into a saucepan; bring slowly to the boil, then remove from heat and leave to infuse for 15 minutes.

Melt the butter or margarine in another saucepan over low heat and then stir in the flour. Gradually add the strained milk, beating well all the time to make a smooth sauce. Bring to the boil, season with salt and pepper. Remove from heat and stir in the minced ingredients and the beaten egg. Pour the mixture into a greased mould or 15 cm (6 in.) baking dish. Cover with a piece of greased foil or greaseproof paper.

Set the mould in a roasting or baking pan with 1 cup of cold water and place it in the centre of a moderately slow oven (160°C; 320°F) and bake for 1 hour. The pâté is cooked when a stainless steel skewer inserted comes away clean. Leave the pâté until it is quite cold, then run a little melted butter or ghee over the surface to keep it moist, and store in the refrigerator. This pâté may be frozen.

Pork and Liver Pâté

8 thin rashers of bacon
500 g (1 lb) pork or chicken liver
500 g (1 lb) pork and veal mince
1 clove garlic
1 teaspoon chopped thyme
2 teaspoons salt
1 teaspoon pepper
2 tablespoons dry white wine or stock

Trim the bacon rashers, discarding any gristle. Stretch them out and use them to line a 4-to-6-cup loaf tin or an 18 cm (8 in.) mould.

Chop the liver and combine with the pork-and-veal mince. Crush the garlic and add with the thyme, salt and pepper to the chopped meat. Mix very thoroughly and add the wine or stock. Spoon the mixture into the centre of the prepared mould and fold the top edges of the bacon rashers into the centre. Cover with buttered paper and kitchen foil.

If possible, allow the mixture to stand for 2 hours before baking to allow the flavours to blend. Place the mould in a roasting pan with 1 cup of cold water. Set in the centre of a moderate oven (180°C; 360°F) and bake for 1½ hours. Remove from heat, pour away any excess liquid fat and cover with fresh papers, placing a weight on top. Leave overnight in a refrigerator or cool place until the pâté is quite firm.

28

BARBECUE PICNICS

With our great interest in barbecuing, many famililes have a portable barbecue or a Japanese hibachi which can be easily transported to a picnic spot in the boot of the car together with charcoal beads, wood or a gas cylinder. An important thing to remember when having a barbecue picnic is the time it takes for the fire to reach the glowing stage suitable for barbecuing. It's always a good idea to have something already prepared for the hungry picnickers to nibble on while they're waiting (see 'Fish and Starters').

I find that Greek lamb kebabs are excellent for picnic barbecues.

Barbecued Trout

Some of the most enjoyable picnics I can recall involved catching trout and barbecuing them at the river bank. Now that trout are farmed so successfully, it is no longer a matter of 'first catch your trout'; you can buy the fish en route or take them out of your freezer. They will have defrosted by lunchtime.

1 trout per person
125 g (4 oz) butter
Salt and pepper
2 teaspoons parsley and dried herbs
A little vegetable oil

Clean the trout, but leave the head on. Combine the butter, salt, pepper and herbs, and place half inside the trout. Rub a little of the flavoured butter over the skin, and oil the rack of the barbecue. Grill for about 5 minutes, then turn and cook for another 5 minutes. Test with the point of a sharp knife.

Remove from the barbecue, season, and top with remaining flavoured butter.

Fruit Kebabs

When the fire has died down, why not make this favourite. You can use various kind of fruit, which you prepare just before barbecuing.

½ rockmelon, peeled and cut into cubes
½ pineapple, peeled, cored and cubed
3 bananas, quartered
¼ – ⅓ cup melted butter
2 tablespoons rum or brown sugar
Juice of 1 orange

Place the prepared fruit in a bowl, and pour over the melted butter and rum. Thread onto skewers. Barbecue, turning and brushing frequently until the fruit is golden and hot.

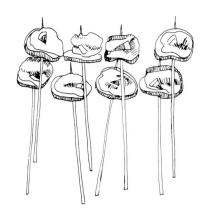

❧ COOK'S NOTES: *Bring meats, poultry*
and fish to room temperature before
cooking. This will give you much more tender
flesh.

SALADS

Greek Lamb Kebabs

½ cup olive oil
½ cup lemon juice or white wine
1 onion, peeled and finely chopped
2 cloves garlic, crushed
2 teaspoons dried oregano or rigani
2 bay leaves
1.5 kg (3 lb) boneless lamb (the shoulder is
 a good cut)
Lemon quarters
Salt and pepper

Combine the oil, lemon juice, onion,
garlic, and dried herbs and beat well.

Cut the lamb into 3–4 cm (2 in.)
cubes and place in a plastic bowl. Pour
the marinade over the meat cubes, add
the bay leaves, cover the bowl and store
in the refrigerator until you are ready to
set off to the picnic. They can be made
the night before.

Thread the cubes onto steel skewers,
pushing the cubes together. Grill
them over glowing coals, turning and
brushing them with the marinade from
time to time.

When the lamb is a good brown
colour on the outside—this takes about
10 minutes—test a cube. If it is cooked
to your taste, season the remainder with
salt and pepper and serve the skewers
with lemon quarters. Pita bread is very
good with skewered meat. Serves 8.

Greek lamb kebabs sizzling over the hot coals.
I have threaded bay leaves on the skewers to give
them an extra pungency.

Kedgeree Salad

This is an excellent dish for a picnic. It
can be made either the morning of the
picnic—as it does not need to be
chilled—or the day before and stored in
a plastic serving bowl overnight in the
refrigerator.

1 tablespoon salad oil
½ onion, finely chopped
2 teaspoons curry powder or to taste
1 cup long-grain rice
2 cups stock or water, heated
500 g (1 lb) smoked fillet of fish
Milk and water
250 g (8 oz) small prawns, peeled
 (optional)
1 can anchovy fillets
3 hard-boiled eggs, peeled
Grated rind and juice of 1 lemon
1 cup sour cream
Chopped parsley

Heat the oil in a heavy saucepan, fry
the onion till golden, add the curry
powder, cook for a few minutes, then
stir in the rice until it glistens. Add the
hot stock, stir well, season to taste with
salt and pepper, cover and cook for
15 minutes or until the rice is tender
and the liquid is absorbed. Allow to
cool. Then fork into a bowl.

Place the fish in the pan, cover with
half milk and half water and poach until
the fish is tender. Drain and remove
any skin or bones, then flake. Add to
the rice, with peeled prawns if using,
4 chopped anchovy fillets, roughly
chopped eggs and grated lemon rind to
taste, and gently mix. Add the lemon

31

juice to the sour cream, then the finely chopped parsley, and gently fold through the salad. Season to taste and decorate with anchovy fillets. Serves 6.

Coleslaw Dressing

Here is an old-fashioned salad dressing that is good for dressing cabbage. It can be carried to the picnic location in a screw-topped jar and mixed with the cabbage at the last minute.

2 tablespoons flour
2 tablespoons sugar
2 teaspoons dry mustard
1 teaspoon salt
6 tablespoons vinegar
6 teaspoons butter or margarine
2 egg yolks
1 cup cream
A pinch of cayenne

Mix the flour, sugar, mustard and salt in a small, heavy saucepan. Blend in the vinegar and cook over low heat, stirring continuously, until the mixture comes to the boil. Allow to cool. Beat in the butter, egg yolks and lastly the cream, until fluffy and well blended. Add the cayenne—and, if too thick, a little more vinegar. For extra rich dressing you can use sour cream. Pour into a screw-top jar and store in the refrigerator.

Pickled Red Cabbage

Red cabbage makes a popular pickle, and it is usually plentiful in the winter months. Choose a young, firm, well-coloured cabbage. Remove the coarse outside leaves and white stalks. Shred finely. Put it in a large basin with layers of salt, and leave it for 24 hours. Drain the cabbage and press out any liquid, rinse thoroughly. Pack it loosely into wide-mouthed jars, cover with cold spiced vinegar (see recipe). This pickle is ready in a week, and it should be eaten while it is still crisp. After 2 to 3 months it becomes too soft and no longer crunchy.

SPICED VINEGAR
5 cups white vinegar
1 teaspoon celery seeds
1 teaspoon mustard seeds
A piece of cinnamon stick
1 teaspoon peppercorns
A piece of fresh ginger
1 teaspoon whole allspice
1 cup sugar

Place all the ingredients for spiced vinegar in a stainless steel or enamel saucepan and bring to the boil. Cover, turn off the heat, and use when cold.

German Potato Salad

This is a particularly good salad to serve with barbecued sausages or frankfurters or cold corned beef. For the best results, use waxy potatoes and serve at room temperature.

6 medium potatoes
1 onion, finely chopped
1 cup chicken stock
4 tablespoons white vinegar
5 tablespoons salad oil
2 teaspoons prepared German mustard
Salt and freshly ground white pepper
½ cup sour cream
Parsley or other fresh herbs to garnish

Boil the potatoes in their skins until just tender. Drain. Peel the potatoes while they are still hot and cut them into slices. Place them in a bowl with the onion. Bring the stock to the boil with the vinegar; and while this is boiling, pour it over the potatoes.

Leave to marinate until almost all the liquid is absorbed—about 20 minutes. Pour off any excess liquid, then gently fold in the oil and mustard mixed together. Taste, and season with salt and pepper if necessary. Lastly, fold in the sour cream. Serve at room temperature, garnished with parsley or other fresh herbs. Serves 6 to 8.

German potato salad garnished with fresh dill.

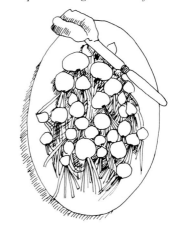

33

Waldorf Coleslaw

Crisp, interesting salads are always welcome at picnics. I shred cabbage in my plastic shredder.

1 small cabbage, shredded
4 spring onions, chopped, including some
    green tops
2 sticks celery, chopped
1 green capsicum (pepper), cored, seeded and
    chopped
1 Granny Smith apple, cored and chopped
½ cup sultanas
¼ cup mayonnaise
¼ cup sour cream
½ cup walnut pieces

DRESSING
1 tablespoon wine vinegar
Salt and freshly ground black pepper
2 teaspoons Dijon mustard
2½ tablespoons olive oil

Put cabbage, spring onions, celery, capsicum (pepper) and apple into a salad bowl and add the sultanas. Whisk together the dressing ingredients, add to the bowl, and mix lightly. Cover and refrigerate for 2 to 3 hours. At serving time, add the mayonnaise and sour cream, sprinkle with walnuts, and toss. Serves 8.

Norfolk Island Salad

This easily prepared salad comes from that lovely semi-tropical island where avocados are plentiful. It can be made at the picnic. Take the dressing in a screw-top jar.

1 soft butterhead or mignonette lettuce
2 ripe but firm avocados
3 kiwi fruit
1½ cups bean sprouts, tipped and tailed
¼ cup fresh coriander leaves

Waldorf coleslaw is a refreshing crunchy dish for a summer picnic.

GINGER DRESSING
2 teaspoons honey
1 tablespoon fresh shredded ginger
1 tablespoon balsamic vinegar or other good
  wine vinegar
1 tablespoon lime or lemon juice
½ cup light olive oil
¼ teaspoon salt
Pepper

Tear the lettuce into bite-sized pieces and arrange on salad plates. Halve the avocados, remove the stones and skin, and cut the flesh into slices. Arrange over lettuce. Peel the kiwi fruit, cut into quarters, and arrange on plates. Strew over bean sprouts and coriander leaves.

Combine the dressing ingredients, shake in a jar, and drizzle over the salads. Serves 4 to 6.

Lentil Salad

The texture and smoky flavour of lentils goes with crunchy sprouts and red onion. In this salad the flavour is enhanced with orange and balsamic vinegar and fresh coriander.

1 cup brown lentils
1½ cups mung bean sprouts
¼ cup chopped red onion
¼ cup orange juice
2 tablespoons olive oil
1 tablespoon balsamic vinegar
1 teaspoon grated orange rind
1 teaspoon ground cumin
1 teaspoon salt
Pepper
½ cup coarsely chopped fresh coriander or
  mint

Boil the lentils in a saucepan of lightly salted water until just tender, about 30 minutes. Drain and rinse well under cold water. Drain again and pat dry. Place in a salad bowl with the remaining ingredients except coriander. Toss well, cover and chill for several hours. Toss in the fresh coriander or mint to serve. Serves 4 to 6.

Brown Rice and Corn Salad

Like all rice salads, this one is better served at room temperature. It is excellent for a picnic, satisfying served alone and particularly delicious with cold chicken.

2 cups brown rice
2 teaspoons French mustard
Salt and pepper
1½ tablespoons lemon juice or white wine
  vinegar
4 tablespoons light olive oil
½ cup mayonnaise or sour cream
3 stalks celery, sliced
½ bunch spring onions, thinly sliced
1 small red capsicum (pepper), seeded and
  diced
3 tablespoons snipped basil leaves
1 cup cooked corn kernels

Bring 4 cups of salted water to the boil in a heavy saucepan. Meanwhile, wash the rice thoroughly, then sprinkle it into the boiling water, so that the water remains at the boil. Boil for a few minutes, then cover tightly. Turn heat to very low and cook without lifting the lid for about 55 minutes.

Remove from heat, uncover for a few minutes to allow the steam to escape, then fluff up with a fork. Cool to room temperature and transfer to a bowl.

Blend the mustard, salt, pepper and lemon juice or vinegar in a small bowl.

Slowly whisk in the oil, combine with the mayonnaise or sour cream. Toss the rice with the dressing. Add the celery, spring onions, diced capsicum, basil, and corn. Toss well and season with salt and pepper if necessary. Serves 8.

Yoghurt Raita (Sauce)

The very best accompaniment to spicy meals is a yoghurt sauce. It is easily made and can be varied according to what is on hand. This recipe uses fresh coriander leaves as a garnish, but you can substitute chopped fresh or dried mint, and you can turn it into a salad with a variety of grated vegetables.

1½ cups natural yoghurt
½ cup cucumber, cut into matchstick strips
1 small onion, peeled and chopped
1 small tomato, chopped
1 teaspoon salt
2 teaspoons chopped coriander leaves
½ teaspoon chilli powder

Put the yoghurt, cucumber, onion, tomato and salt in a bowl and stir well to mix. Sprinkle with the coriander leaves and chilli powder, cover, and then chill in the refrigerator until ready to transport. It is best made the day you aim to eat it.

Bean Sprout Salad

500 g (1 lb) bean sprouts
2 tablespoons soy sauce
1 teaspoon sugar
A few drops of sesame oil

Remove tails from sprouts. Rinse in cold water, drain. Transfer to a bowl.

Combine the soy sauce, sugar and sesame oil. Pour over the bean sprouts and toss gently. Cover and refrigerate. Serves 4 to 6.

VARIATIONS: For the sesame oil, substitute 1½ tablespoons peanut oil. Add 1 tablespoon vinegar to the dressing.

Tabouleh-stuffed Capsicums (Peppers)

Tabouleh-stuffed capsicums are a favourite of a vegetarian group I've seen at a nearby harbourside park, and they kindly gave me the recipe.

1 cup burghul (cracked wheat)
8 small green capsicums (peppers)
½ cup olive oil
¼ cup lemon juice
¼ cup chopped fresh mint
¼ cup chopped parsley
2 teaspoons salt
Freshly ground black pepper
2 cups alfalfa sprouts
1 cup peeled, seeded, chopped cucumber
2 tomatoes, chopped
½ cup chopped spring onions

Soak burghul in water overnight in a glass or ceramic bowl. Drain and squeeze out as much water as possible, then spread out on a tea-towel for 30 minutes. Blanch the capsicums in boiling salted water for 5 minutes. Drain and refresh under cold running water. Cut off tops, discard seeds and ribs and let the capsicums drain. Combine the oil, lemon juice, herbs, salt and remaining ingredients. Stuff the capsicums with the mixture, mounding it high, and arrange them in a dish deep enough to hold them upright. Serves 8.

Carrot and pecan salad ready to be served on cos lettuce leaves. It is fun to eat with fingers at a picnic.

Carrot and Pecan Salad

This is a variation of a popular French salad—carrot and walnut. I have substituted pecans for the walnuts as they store better than walnuts.

2 cups shredded carrots
½ cup raisins
6–8 pecan halves, chopped
1 lettuce—mignonette, cos or butterhead

DRESSING
2 tablespoons olive oil
2 teaspoons hazelnut or walnut oil
    (optional)
1 tablespoon lemon juice
Salt and pepper

Combine the shredded carrots, raisins and pecans in a bowl. Moisten with dressing made by shaking the ingredients for the dressing in a screw-top jar.

Serve on washed and crisp lettuce leaves on individual plates or on one serving dish. Serves 6.

Black-Eyed Pea Salad

These dried white beans, called peas in America, with their characteristic black splotch, have become a favourite food for health-seeking grain eaters. They are obtainable at health food shops and make excellent salads.

1 cup black-eyed peas
½ teaspoon salt
1 tablespoon white wine vinegar
A few dashes of Tabasco or chilli powder
¼ cup olive oil or other salad oil
½ cup finely chopped red onion
2 tomatoes, peeled and diced
1 stick celery, sliced
¼ cup finely chopped parsley
Pepper and salt to taste

Rinse the peas under a cold tap, place in a bowl and cover generously with boiling water; let them soak for an hour. Drain the peas, rinse again under the cold tap, and put them into a saucepan with enough water to cover them by 5 cm (2 in.).

Simmer the peas, removing any froth, for about 20 minutes, then add the salt and simmer until the peas are tender. The cooking time will vary, but about a further 10 minutes should do.

Drain the peas, rinse under water. Place in a serving bowl. Combine the vinegar, Tabasco or chilli and oil and beat until creamy; pour over the peas with the onion, tomatoes, celery and parsley. Season to taste with salt and pepper. Serves 6.

French Barley Salad

Although more widely used for brewing than eating, barley has a pleasant nutty flavour and makes delicious salads. Pearl barley, the polished grain, is more widely available than Scotch barley and will cook to tenderness in about an hour or so.

2 cups pearl barley
1 large cucumber
8 radishes
2 sticks celery
2–4 spring onions
½ cup chopped coriander, or ½ cup parsley
   chopped with a few sprigs of mint
Salt and pepper
1 small lettuce
Coriander sprigs to garnish

DRESSING
3 tablespoons lemon juice
1 teaspoon salt
1 teaspoon cumin
½ cup olive oil

Cover the barley with cold water in a saucepan and bring to the boil. Remove from heat, cover, and stand for 1 hour. Drain, cover again with salted cold water, bring to the boil and simmer until tender, about 1 to 1½ hours. Drain and toss gently with dressing (see below). Set aside till cool.

Peel, seed and chop the cucumber, slice the radishes and celery, and shred the spring onions. Add the coriander or parsley and mint, toss with the barley, and season with salt and pepper to taste. Chill until ready to transport. Garnish with coriander sprigs. Serves 6.

DRESSING: Put the lemon juice, salt and cumin into a small bowl. Add olive oil little by little, beating with a fork or whisk.

BREAD, CAKES AND BISCUITS

Soda Bread with Herbs

Although the Irish are renowned as bakers of soda bread, here is a popular herbed loaf made by Scottish housewives, who always grew parsley and chives outside their cottage door.

Soda bread with herbs is a perfect bread to take on a picnic. It can be made the day before and will still be fresh and moist on the day. It is firm and won't deteriorate with transporting.

2 cups wholemeal flour
2 cups plain flour
2 teaspoons salt
2 teaspoons sugar
1 teaspoon bicarbonate of soda
¾ teaspoon baking powder
90 g (3 oz) butter
½ cup chopped parsley
1 tablespoon snipped chives
1 tablespoon chopped fresh rosemary or
    1 teaspoon dried
2 cups buttermilk

Sift the flours, salt, sugar, soda and baking powder into a large bowl. Rub in the butter until the mixture resembles breadcrumbs. Stir in the herbs, then the buttermilk, and mix to a soft dough.

Place on a greased baking tray and, with floured hands, form into a 20 cm (8 in.) round. Using a sharp, floured knife, cut a cross 1 cm ($\frac{1}{2}$ in.) deep in the top. Bake in a preheated moderately hot oven (190°C; 375°F) for 40 to 45 minutes or until the loaf sounds hollow when tapped on the bottom. Serve warm or at room temperature, sliced.

Citrus Tea Bread

This is a combination of three great flavours, Earl Grey tea, lemon and nuts.

2 teaspoons or 1 teabag Earl Grey tea
$\frac{1}{2}$ cup boiling water
60 g (2 oz) butter
$\frac{3}{4}$ cup sugar
1 egg, lightly beaten
1 tablespoon grated orange rind
1 teaspoon grated lemon rind
3 cups flour
1 teaspoon baking powder
1 teaspoon bicarbonate of soda
$\frac{1}{2}$ teaspoon salt
$\frac{1}{2}$ teaspoon cinnamon
$\frac{3}{4}$ cup orange juice
$\frac{1}{2}$ cup chopped walnuts

Mix the tea with the boiling water. Leave it to steep for 3 minutes, then strain if using loose tealeaves. Cream the butter and sugar until light and fluffy. Add the egg and rinds and beat

A water view is a must for many picnickers. The citrus tea bread here has just been cut for eating.

well. Sift the flour, baking power, bicarbonate of soda, salt and cinnamon. Add to the butter mixture with the juice and the tea. Stir gently, then mix in the nuts.

Turn the mixture into a greased and lined 21 × 15 cm (8 × 6 in.) loaf tin. Bake in a preheated moderate oven (180°C; 360°F) for 45 minutes or until a skewer inserted in the centre comes out clean. Cool completely before serving.

Barabrith

A welsh fruit bread packed with flavour.

2 cups self-raising flour
A pinch of salt
1 teaspoon mixed spice
60 g (2 oz) butter
$\frac{1}{3}$ cup sugar
Grated rind of 1 lemon
$\frac{3}{4}$ cup sultanas
$\frac{1}{4}$ cup treacle
1 egg, beaten
$\frac{1}{2}$ teaspoon bicarbonate of soda
$\frac{1}{2}$ cup milk

Sift the flour, salt and spice into a bowl. Rub in the butter until the mixture resembles fine breadcrumbs. Stir in the sugar, lemon rind and sultanas. Add the treacle and egg. Dissolve the bicarbonate of soda in the milk, add to the flour mixture, and mix until well blended. Turn into a greased and lined 21 × 15 cm (8 × 6 in.) loaf tin. Bake in a preheated moderate oven (180°C; 360°F) for about 1$\frac{1}{4}$ hours or until a skewer inserted in the centre comes out clean. Turn onto a wire rack to cool. Wrap the loaf in foil and store it for 24 hours before serving, sliced and buttered.

Cupcakes

Individual butter cakes in paper cups are just the thing for a family picnic. They can be made ahead and stored in the freezer. They take about 30 minutes to thaw.

125 g (4 oz) butter
¾ cup castor sugar
1 teaspoon vanilla essence
2 large eggs, beaten
2 cups self-raising flour
A pinch of salt
⅔ cup milk
Whipped cream
Icing sugar

Line patty tins with paper cases. Cream the butter and gradually add the sugar, beating until smooth and creamy. Add the vanilla and the eggs gradually, beating well after each addition. Sift the flour with the salt and fold lightly into the creamed mixture alternately with the milk. Spoon the mixture into the paper cases until three-quarters full. Bake in a moderately hot oven (190°C; 375°F) for approximately 15 minutes. Makes 24 cakes.

COOK'S NOTES: *Everyone has a favourite spot for a picnic—by the sea, under leafy trees, by a rushing steam or in a hidden glen. Some of us like to commune with nature, cook over an open fire and eat with our fingers, while others spread tablecloths and bring out their fine glass, china and silver.*

Pineapple Boiled Fruit Cake

Just as no tea-table in elegant England was complete without a plum cake, no picnic in Australia is complete without a fruit loaf. This is a particularly easy one to cook. The addition of crushed pineapple helps to keep it moist to the last crumb.

500 g (1 lb) mixed fruit
1 cup brown sugar
150 g (5 oz) butter
440 g (14 oz) can crushed pineapple
2 eggs, lightly beaten
1 cup plain flour
1 cup self-raising flour
1 teaspoon mixed spice
¼ teaspoon bicarbonate of soda

Place the mixed fruit, sugar, butter and can of crushed pineapple—including the juice—in a saucepan. Stir well, bring to the boil, lower heat and simmer very gently for 5 minutes. Cool thoroughly and add the beaten eggs.

Sift the remaining ingredients into a large bowl and beat in the fruit mixture. Place the mixture in a greased and lined 20 cm (8 in.) square tin or a large loaf tin and bake in a moderately slow oven (160°C; 320°F) for 1¾ hours—test by inserting a skewer after 1½ hours (if it comes out clean, the cake is cooked). When cooked, remove the cake from the oven and stand it on a cooling rack. When it is cold, turn it out of the tin and store in a cake tin. This cake is easier to slice when stored for a few days.

Carrot Cookies

Very popular with children, these healthy biscuits contain very little sugar and depend on the grated carrot for sweetness.

Carrot cookies don't last long at a picnic. They're easy to make and transport.

2 cups flour
2 teaspoons baking powder
½ teaspoon salt
250 g (8 oz) butter or margarine, softened
¼ cup sugar
1 egg
1 teaspoon vanilla essence
2 cups grated raw carrot
¼ cup chopped nuts
¼ cup wheat germ

Lightly grease several baking trays. Sift the flour with the baking powder and salt, set aside. In the large bowl of an electric mixer, at medium speed, cream the butter or margarine until soft, then gradually add the sugar and beat until light and fluffy. Add the egg and vanilla essence, mix well.

At low speed, beat in the flour mixture, then the grated carrot, nuts and wheat germ, beating just until they are combined.

Drop by teaspoonfuls. 5 cm (2 in.) apart, on greased baking trays. Bake in moderate oven (180°C; 360°F) for 20 to 25 minutes. Remove the cooked biscuits to a wire rack. Makes 36. Store in an airtight container when cool. I always save the attractive biscuit tins which come as Christmas presents. They are so useful for storing and transporting home-made biscuits.

Coconut Biscuits

These delicate biscuits are very easy to make; but take care not to overheat the butter, and leave enough room between the biscuits when setting them out on the baking trays.

180 g (6 oz) butter
¾ cup castor sugar
1 egg

1 teaspoon vanilla
2½ cups self-raising flour
¾ cup desiccated coconut

Place the butter in a mixing bowl and stand it over hot water until the butter has just melted; allow it to cool a little, then stir in the sugar, beaten egg and vanilla. Mix well. Sift the flour over the top of the mixture, then add the coconut and stir until combined. Form into walnut-sized balls and place on lightly greased biscuit trays, leaving room for the mixture of spread; with a drinking glass, press each ball lightly to flatten it slightly. Bake in a moderate oven (180°C; 360°F) for 15 minutes or until a pale golden colour.

Plums in Red Wine Sauce

When plums are cheap and plentiful, this is an excellent way of preserving them. Store them in the refrigerator until you go on your picnic.

2 kg (4 lb) plums
3 cups water
1 cup sugar
1 stick cinnamon
1 cup red wine

Wash the plums well under a running tap. Bring the water and sugar slowly to the boil, and boil for 5 minutes. Add the cinnamon, wine and plums, and gently simmer the fruit about 5 minutes until tender, taking care not to break the skins. Remove the plums with a slotted spoon, and put them in screw-top jars, then bring the remaining syrup to boiling point, top the plums with the boiling syrup, and over the jars with closely fitting lids. When cold, store the jars in the refrigerator. When covering fruit syrup containing wine, make sure the screw-top lids are lacquered or made of plastic.

FRUIT

Fruit is the happiest ending to a picnic. And the popular fruit when it is in season is the watermelon. The greengrocer will cut you a piece if the melon is large. Don't cut it into slices until you get to the picnic.

For the sweet tooth, a rockmelon is a favourite, especially if you cut a round plug from the stem, remove the seeds, sprinkle the inside with 2 tablespoons of sugar, and pour in $\frac{1}{2}$ cup of port or sweet sherry. Replace the plug and wrap the melon in plastic film and chill.

Pears, apples, bananas and apricots are all good picnic food.

DRINKS FOR A PICNIC

Cool, frosty drinks, cold beer, chilled wines and hot tea or coffee will all be appreciated at a picnic. What you decide on depends on the time of the year, whether you can light a fire, the age of your guests and the amount of ice you can take with you. If you plan to make tea or coffee at the picnic, remember to take water, sugar, milk and mugs.

The easiest drinks for young children are the small packs of fruit juice which come complete with a straw. The packs can be frozen overnight in the freezer and will help to keep the contents of the picnic basket cool.

Beer in cans is a popular drink and can usually be bought en route to the picnic. But the most popular drink with the ladies is surely Buck's Fizz, and with champagne available at a price to suit every pocket, it is a winner.

Barley Lemonade

This refreshing drink, popular in Victorian times, is enjoying a revival today. It keeps well in the refrigerator and when bottled and chilled is easy to transport.

⅓ cup pearl barley
5 cups water
A pinch of salt
2 or 3 lemons, juice and strips of rind
Sugar or honey to taste

Wash the barley and put it into a heavy saucepan with the water, salt and lemon rind. Allow to boil, then simmer slowly for 2 hours. Strain into a large jug and allow to cool. Strain the lemon juice and add to the barley water with sugar or honey to taste. Add more lemon juice if desired. Makes 6 cups.

Fresh Bitter Lemon Crush

Serve this light and refreshing drink in addition to wine.

Peel and chop 3 lemons and an orange into chunks, discarding peel, then blend in a food processor or blender until pulpy. Add icing sugar to taste and either some sprigs of lemon balm or mint or a few drops of Angostura Bitters. Strain through a sieve, rubbing well with a ladle. When you've squeezed as much juice as possible from the pulp, discard it. Transport the juice concentrated, ready to dilute with chilled sparkling mineral water.

Barley lemonade tastes so good it is hard to believe it is also good for you.

Buck's Fizz

1 bottle of inexpensive champagne or sparkling white wine
1 litre cartoon of orange juice

Have both the champagne and orange juice well chilled, then pack in insulated bags or next to the ice packs in the picnic basket. When ready to serve, mix 1 part wine to 1 part orange or as you like it.

Mulled Wine

For a winter picnic, mulled wine is a popular thirst quencher.

1 bottle red wine
2 tablespoons sugar
1 stick cinnamon, crumbled
4 cloves
1 lemon
2 oranges

Pour the wine into a saucepan with the sugar, cinnamon, cloves and the thinly pared rind of the lemon and the oranges. Heat slowly, stirring occasionally, and add the strained juice of the lemon and oranges. Do not allow to boil. Mulled wine can be prepared at the picnic or made at home and poured into a warmed vacuum flask. Don't forget a corkscrew if you intend making it at the picnic.

COOK'S NOTES: *Don't pollute water, and respect the wildlife, the flowers, shrubs and trees. Take along some guide books and teach your children to identify the birds or flowers, so they learn to live in harmony with nature.*

47

INDEX

Page numbers in **bold** type indicate illustrations.